young
CHANGEMAKERS
DREAM CHASERS

Written By
STACY C. BAUER

Illustrated By
EMANUELA NTAMACK

This book is dedicated to Isabel, Melati, London, Brayden, Arren, Adom, Ayla, Shai Ann, Hayley, Shlok, Jade, Bria, Livia, Molly and Kaitlyn. Keep chasing your dreams.

Dream Chasers
Young Change Makers
Published by Hop Off the Press, LLC
www.stacycbauer.com

Minneapolis, MN

Editing by Lor Bingham and Chelsea Tornetto.
Book design by Travis D. Peterson.

Library of Congress Control Number: 2022911086
Bauer, Stacy C. Author
Ntamack, Emanuela Illustrator
Dream Chasers

ISBN: 979-8-9867584-2-8

JUVENILE NONFICTION

All inquiries of this book can be sent to the author.
For more information, please visit **www.stacycbauer.com**

MEET THE CHANGE MAKERS!

HELPING HANDS
Delivering support to those in need.

INSPIRATIONAL ICONS
Chasing their dreams and
encouraging others to do the same!

ANIMAL AMBASSADORS
Helping and advocating for animals.

CONSERVATION CREW
Saving the planet.

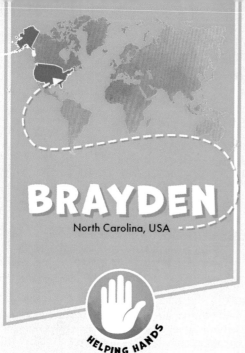

BRAYDEN

North Carolina, USA

HELPING HANDS

"DOING GOOD FOR OTHERS HAS A WAY OF COMING BACK TO YOU."

You may think a five-year-old can't do anything to change the world, but you'd be wrong. When Brayden Frasure was five years old, something happened that changed the direction of his life forever.

Brayden was out with his family when a homeless woman asked for some spare change. Although his family did not have any change, his mom used her debit card to buy the woman a sandwich. Brayden never forgot that moment of helping someone in need and decided to take action.

Some of the first things Brayden did were small things for him, but made big differences for the people he helped. When he and his family went out to eat, they would give leftover food or carry-out meals to people who needed it. Whenever he saw someone experiencing homelessness, he asked his mom to stop and get them food. During the COVID-19 pandemic, Brayden packed bags with food and clothing to give to the local homeless shelter. Brayden's ultimate goal was to buy a food truck and use that to feed people in need.

To fund the food truck, he saved up money he earned from acting in movies, television shows and commercials. When he appeared on the television show *Little Big Shots*, actress Kristin Bell gave him $5,000 too. He was then able to use that money to design and buy his food truck! He drew pictures of what he wanted on each side of the truck. Those pictures included Bible verses he thought would inspire people, a chalkboard menu, his logo and the names of his sponsors. A business called The Print Path then turned his design into a wrap for the truck for free!

Brayden has many uses for his food truck. He travels to the homeless shelter in his city a few times each month to feed the people there. Brayden and his family do events at churches or festivals to raise money to purchase more food. He accepts only donations for the food at these events, then uses those donations to purchase more food for the homeless shelter and for his food truck! He also uses his food truck to help raise money for people experiencing an

illness. Any donations he receives on a certain day, he will then give to the person who is sick.

Brayden saw a need and took a small step to help meet that need. With the help of his family, friends and community and his own hard work, passion and determination, Brayden took bigger and bigger steps. He wants you to know that you can make a difference too!

5

BRAYDEN'S FUN FACTS:

- Brayden is an actor.
- He loves to sing karaoke and play the piano.
- He loves water activities on the lake.

young
CHANGEMAKERS™
HELPING HAND!

- Visit or call a homeless shelter in your area and see how you can help.
- Keep a box of granola bars and bottled water in your car. If you see a person in need, give them some food and water.

But Donations are apprecia to help me feed the homele

For I was hungry and you gave me something to eat, I was thirsty and you gave me something to drink, I was a stranger and you invited me in. –Matthew 25:35

MY STORY

MENU

BRAYDEN'S ADVICE FOR YOU:
Do good things for God and others, not for yourself or your own fame and respect.

MOLLY & KAITLYN

Pennsylvania, USA

INSPIRATIONAL ICONS

GNN
GOOD NEWS NOW

"LOOK FOR THE GOOD THAT'S OUT THERE."

Do you ever watch or read the news? Taking in too much negative news can make people tired, anxious, depressed and even cause stomach problems.

Molly and Kaitlyn Harrington noticed people were feeling down because of everything going on in the world, specifically during the COVID-19 pandemic, and wanted to do something to raise people's spirits. They learned that hearing inspiring things makes people happier. So, they decided to try to find and share uplifting stories with the world.

The sisters asked their dad to record their news broadcast and started seeking out positive news. They reported about people making face masks, and bakeries delivering treats to hospital workers. They shared the video on social media. They planned on only doing it once or twice, but after seeing the positive reaction, it turned into a weekly broadcast—They called it Good News Now (GNN). They kept reporting on positive news including rediscovered species thought to be extinct, and people planting millions of trees.

Now, they have a segment called GNN Heartfelt Heroes which features people in their community who are helping others. The stories include people who have cooked meals for Ukrainian refugees, fixed donated cars and given them to families in need, and given free haircuts to the homeless. Another one of their segments is GNN Kind Kids, which features kids who are helping their communities. Some stories they have reported on include kids helping stray animals get adopted, children who are running marathons to raise money for veterans, and a girl who is building wheelchairs for disabled pets.

Their community helps them by sharing their broadcasts on social media, sharing positive news with them and encouraging them to keep the show going. People around the world have told Molly and Kaitlyn that they look forward to their weekly positive news show. Their show is seen in over 60 countries and is shown in 25 different Facebook groups that focus on happiness, positivity and good news!

When the girls began their journey, they had some self-doubt. They weren't sure they could make a difference or if anyone would watch the show. Molly worked hard to get comfortable reading her script in front of the camera. It was a challenge getting the word out about their show and finding people to watch it, but as their journey continued, their self-confidence grew. They both plan on continuing to help people see the good in the world.

KAITLYN'S FUN FACTS:

- Kaitlyn sings in four choral groups for both her school and church.

- She has earned the Girl Scout Gold, Silver and Bronze Awards.

- She has performed in over 25 musical productions like *Cinderella* and *Lion King*.

- She enjoys karate.

MOLLY'S FUN FACTS:

- Molly plays percussion for her school's concert and jazz bands.

- She has won several championships as a softball pitcher.

- She has acted in several musicals, including *Beauty and the Beast* and *Annie*.

- She plays volleyball.

BECOME A

 young CHANGEMAKERS™ INSPIRATIONAL ICON!

MOLLY'S ADVICE FOR YOU:

If you want to make a difference, just start with a small first step. Small steps make big differences.

KAITLYN'S ADVICE FOR YOU:

There is so much good in our communities that is often overlooked. Once you start doing good, others will join you.

- Focus on the good in the world. Look for the people helping others.

- Be a helper.

- Share good news with others.

Kaitlyn   *Molly*

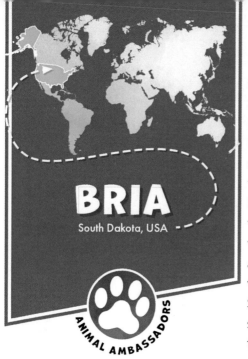

BRIA

South Dakota, USA

ANIMAL AMBASSADORS

"START SMALL, BUT THINK BIG."

Did you know that over 40,000 **species** of plants and animals around the world are threatened by extinction? In the last 500 years, human activity has forced over 800 species into extinction. We have taken over the creatures' habitats, hunted them, and harmed them with pollution. When Bria Shay was eight years old, she learned about **endangered** animals and wanted to do something to help. She believes that everyone can do something to help if they use their talents. Bria loves painting and she's good at it, so she decided to use that talent to make a difference by painting endangered animals and selling the paintings.

Bria begins by researching an endangered animal. She studies the animal, watches videos about it and uses books and images to help her decide how she will paint it. Her mom, family, friends and neighbors donate painting supplies. Bria paints on canvas using acrylics, watercolors and graphite. She paints every week and spends a couple of weeks on each painting.

She has learned that art is a great conversation starter and her paintings have done just that. Through her paintings, people have become aware of which animals are endangered and learned more about them. People have been inspired to help by buying Bria's artwork after learning about it on social media and on her website.

Bria sells her paintings at charity auctions, fundraisers, in person and on her website, and donates the money to nonprofit organizations who help endangered species. Through many hours of research, she has found four charities to support.

So far, Bria has raised over $75,000 for endangered an-imals. She has loved meeting kids from all over the world at different events and getting people talking about endangered species. Her goal is to keep doing what she's doing and to ultimately raise $100,000!

A **SPECIES** is a group of similar living things that can have babies.

ENDANGERED species are close to extinction in the wild.

young CHANGEMAKERS™
ANIMAL AMBASSADOR!

- Check out the charities Bria supports: The International Fund For Animal Welfare, The Wolf Conservation Center in New York, The David Shepherd Wildlife Foundation in the UK, and The Jane Goodall Institute.

- Read more about her and see her beautiful paintings at: www.instagram.com/briashayneffofficial

BRIA'S FUN FACTS:

- Bria loves mint chocolate chip ice cream.

- Her favorite colors are purple and mint green.

- She likes rollerblading and hanging out with her dogs and friends.

- Bria's favorite animals are the Mexican gray wolf, red wolf, and cheetah.

BRIA'S ADVICE FOR YOU:

All kids have the ability to change the world. It doesn't matter how old you are or your economic situation. Use your passion, turn it into action and change the world!

JADE

Minnesota, USA

HELPING HANDS

"EVERYONE DESERVES A BEDTIME STORY."

13

Do you like to read? What is your favorite book? Do you have a lot of books? Jade VanWinkle loves to read, but when she was younger, she wasn't always able to find books she was interested in reading at the library and her family couldn't afford to buy new ones. Many times, they would get books at the thrift store. Jade knew there were other kids like her who didn't have enough money to buy new books, so she decided to see if she could help. At age 13, Jade and her mom began a new partnership that would change their lives! They decided to see if they could get books to kids who needed them.

Jade started looking through her books. She set aside the ones she was done reading. She and her mom also visited thrift stores. When their friends and family heard about their new mission to get books into kids' hands, they started donating books too! They called their new mission Books for Better, MN and started Facebook and Instagram pages. Word quickly spread and they received more and more donations!

Jade and her mom spend a lot of time looking for books, cleaning them up, bundling them and finding children who need them. Jade enjoys looking for books for kids her age. She handpicks books for those kids and then her mom drops them off when they're ready. The books they collect go to foster families, shelters, and other local programs. They also give them to kids in their community whose parents request them.

Books for Better, MN has given away over a thousand books. They also host book fairs at a local business. Kids in the community can come and pick out free books. They are also kicking off a new event called Read in the Park. Families can visit local parks for storytime and outdoor fun!

Jade is doing what she can to get books into kids' hands and also get them excited about reading. She wants to keep inspiring kids to follow their dreams and make a difference.

young CHANGEMAKERS™ HELPING HAND!

- Go through your books. Are there some you can donate?

- Visit thrift stores and purchase books to give to Jade's program or a similar program in your area.

- Visit **www.facebook.com/ nj.booksforbetter** to learn more!

JADE'S FUN FACTS:

- Jade enjoys playing softball.

- She loves snowboarding.

- Her favorite color is hot pink.

JADE'S ADVICE FOR YOU:

Don't be afraid to be yourself and do the things that make you happy.

jade

"BE YOURSELF, STAY ALERT."

ADOM
South Carolina, USA

INSPIRATIONAL ICONS

When Adom Appiah was in seventh grade, his history teacher gave his class an assignment: they were to dedicate 20% of their history period each day to a service project. It was called 20Time. They were to find a need that their community had and then work toward a solution. Adom loved sports and believed that sports could unite the community in a positive way. He talked to his parents and his teacher about his idea, thought of a name for the mission, created social media pages and a website, and found a mentor. Ball4Good was born. They are a youth-led nonprofit charity whose goal is to have fun, raise funds and make a positive impact on the community through sports.

Ball4Good's first event was a celebrity basketball game. The purpose was to bring the community together for a fun event and raise funds for a good cause. With help from his mentor and family, Adom recruited celebrities from his community to compete, coach and cheer. He needed some start-up money, so he used the money he received for his 13th birthday. Adom, with the help of his teachers, friends, community members, parents and classmates, began spreading the word about the upcoming game. He charged money for tickets to attend. That first basketball game drew over 800 spectators and $7,500 was able to be donated to the local **Boys & Girls Clubs of America**! This then turned into an annual tradition and became sponsored by local businesses.

Adom has since expanded Ball-4Good to include student leaders who do everything from organize events to decide which charities Ball4Good donates to. His non-profit has also worked with school sports teams to collect food, toys, and clothing during games, which are donated to people experiencing homelessness. They also collected winter hats for cancer patients and held a Christmastime sports equipment drive for kids in their community.

Ball4Good has donated over $100,000 and supported more than 36 organizations. Businesses, adults and students all work together in this mission. Adom's goal is to expand this mission past his community and to continue inspiring other youth to get involved and follow their dreams.

ADOM'S FUN FACTS:

- Adom loves to dance.

- He likes reading and music.

- His favorite food is jollof rice: a West African stew made with rice, chili peppers, and meat or fish.

Are you on a sports team? What can your team do as a group to make a difference in your community?

Check out Adom's books inspiring young people to change the world and bounce back from failure. Donations from book sales support charity.

Visit ball4good.org to learn more about Adom's mission and his books.

ADOM'S ADVICE FOR YOU:
With perseverance and positivity, nearly any end goal can be reached.

Adom

AYLA & SHAI ANN

Colorado, USA

CONSERVATION CREW

Picture your favorite tree. Maybe it's a towering redwood, a swaying palm tree, or a colorful maple. Did you know that there are over 60,000 different types of trees in the world? Trees help our planet, animals and ourselves.

One way trees help our environment is through **photosynthesis**, their food making process. They absorb **carbon dioxide** and store it in their trunks. They take this poisonous gas out of the air for us! Being around trees calms people and makes them happier. Many animals make their homes in trees. They also give us shade and clean water! They are important to people, animals and our earth.

Ayla and Shai Ann Kanow agree. When Ayla was 16 years old, she was hiking Mount Whitney in California with some other students during her summer camp. When Ayla saw how amazed the city kids were by

19

the scenery, she realized that not everyone has access to the beauty of nature. She was inspired to try to create more opportunities for other people to enjoy nature. She also wanted to do something to help the environment, and decided that planting trees was a great way to do that!

In 2020, with the help of their family, Ayla and her sister Shai Ann created a nonprofit they called Seas of Trees. They wanted to get kids involved in helping the environment through planting trees. Today, Seas of Trees partners with local summer camps to educate kids about the importance of trees. They teach the students how they can take action to help the environment. Seas of Trees buys **saplings** and plants them with the students.

Students ages three through 18 come to these summer camps from all over the country. Ayla is passionate about helping these young people build a connection with nature. Through their website, social media, media features and connections in their community, Seas of Trees has planted over 2,500 trees, raised over $7,000, and taken 5,000,000 pounds of carbon dioxide out of the air!

They also donate money to international projects to help them buy saplings native to their ecosystems. They have several planting hubs around the world including in Costa Rica, Nepal, Peru, Guatemala and Colorado. The experience that has changed the sisters the most was partnering with students in Guatemala and Nepal. Each student got paid a day of wages to experience the

PHOTOSYNTHESIS happens when plants use sunlight, water, and carbon dioxide to create oxygen and energy in the form of sugar.

CARBON DIOXIDE is a heavy colorless gas that is formed by burning fuels (mostly coal). People also exhale carbon dioxide when they breathe. When there is too much of it in the air, it traps heat from the sun and raises the earth's temperature. This is called the Greenhouse Effect. Too much carbon dioxide can also cause headaches and dizziness in people.

A **SAPLING** is a young tree.

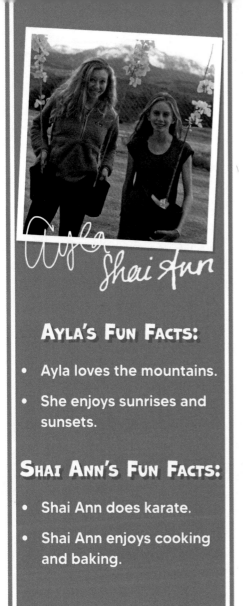

Ayla
Shai Ann

AYLA'S FUN FACTS:

- Ayla loves the mountains.
- She enjoys sunrises and sunsets.

SHAI ANN'S FUN FACTS:

- Shai Ann does karate.
- Shai Ann enjoys cooking and baking.

hands-on job of planting trees. In Guatemala, their organization planted trees on a hill that was damaged by a mudslide, and in Nepal, they planted fruit trees at an all-girls school so, in future years, they will be provided with healthy food.

Seas of Trees plans to keep educating others about the power of trees. The sisters are excited to encourage more and more youth to get involved in planting trees and enjoying nature. They are working toward planting 10,000 trees! Every tree planted makes a difference in the world.

BECOME A  **CONSERVATION CREW MEMBER!**

- **Plant a tree!**
- **Check out their website www.seasoftrees.org for more information.**

AYLA AND SHAI ANN'S ADVICE FOR YOU:

Speak up for what you think is right and do not doubt yourself about how far you can get. Remember that you are passionate about what you are doing, so it does not matter what other people think of you. Encourage others and be proud of what you have created!

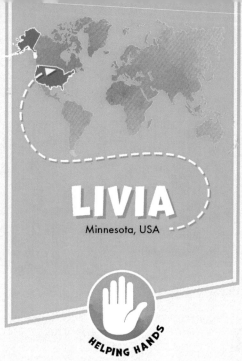

LIVIA
Minnesota, USA

HELPING HANDS

"IN ALL YOUR WAYS ACKNOWLEDGE HIM, AND HE SHALL DIRECT YOUR PATHS."
PROVERBS 3:6

Do you have food allergies? Does anyone you know have them? When Livia Murray was just nine months old, she was diagnosed with severe allergies to peanuts, tree nuts, coconut, sesame, sunflower seeds, peaches and cherries. Since then, she has had to be very careful not to eat any foods containing these **allergens**. When she was little, it was hard going to bakeries or being around treats, so her mom taught her to bake. She doesn't remember a time when she wasn't in the kitchen. In fact, her mom says Livia was helping bake pies when she was just three years old! Livia soon developed a passion for it and started baking for others.

Because Livia knew first-hand how hard it is to find desserts when you have food allergies, she decided to start making birthday cakes and cupcakes for kids with food allergies. She wanted them to have a special treat for their birthday that they could enjoy.

Livia began receiving more and more orders for baked goods. Livia's mom helped her start a business and get a special license from the state of Minnesota so she could bake out of her home and sell the treats. A friend created a

website and logo, which Livia started sharing on social media. Her sisters joined her in baking and they created the company L.I.V. Freely. The name comes from the first initials of her and her sisters' first names, Livia, Isla and Vienna. They used the word "freely" because it describes how Livia wants people to live—free from worrying about their food allergies.

Livia is happy to help others who also have food allergies. She has learned that there are more people with food allergies than she ever imagined. In fact, about 32 million people in the United States alone live with food allergies! Right now, Livia and her sisters bake in their allergen- free kitchen, but someday, they hope to have a storefront. Livia loves seeing the smiles on the kids' faces when she presents them with their allergy-free baked goods. She loves making a difference!

An ALLERGEN is any normally harmless substance that causes an immediate allergic reaction. The eight most common food allergens are milk, eggs, fish, shellfish, tree nuts, peanuts, wheat, and soybeans.

- Visit Livia's website to learn more about her business: livfreelybakedgoods.com

- Be aware of classmates and friends who have food allergies. Don't make fun of them. If you are bringing lunch from home or a class snack, bring something that won't leave them out.

LIVIA'S ADVICE FOR YOU:

If you see a need, take the leap and fill that need! It is beyond rewarding. It doesn't matter what limitations you may think you have, you are able to overcome them.

Livia

LIVIA'S FUN FACTS:

- Livia has been home-schooled for five years.

- She is a huge Disney World fan.

- She loves fashion and photography!

ARREN

North Carolina, USA

INSPIRATIONAL ICONS

"GOD IS GREATER THAN THE UPS AND DOWNS."

Did you know that 10-year-old Dimitrios Loundras was the youngest gymnast ever to compete in the Olympic games? That was back in 1896! Arren Booth is only 10 years old too, but someday she wants to follow in Dimitrios' footsteps.

When Arren's mom first enrolled her in dance class, Arren loved the tumbling part of the class the most. After she had learned all of the gymnastics she could from her dance teachers, they suggested her mom put her in gymnastics. Arren started practicing gymnastics when she was four years old. Now, at age 10, she is competing at level 10, having passed out of or completed all of the other levels. Arren has belonged to a gym and has had the same coach since she was five years old. Arren trains for 30 hours each week and strives toward her goal of competing in the Olympics one day. She manages to balance training with school, since she is home-schooled through a flexible online academy. Arren's plan is to follow the **elite path** and to compete in all four events: vault, bars, beam, and floor.

Arren motivates and encourages her teammates. She always tries

Arren's Fun Facts:

- Arren's favorite food is pizza.

- Her favorite color is blue.

- Her favorite gymnast is **Simone Biles**.

- Arren loves making bracelets and going kayaking in her spare time.

Left: Arren on a balance beam. Right: Simone Biles at the 2016 Olympics all-around gold medal podium. Biles photo by Materialscientist is licensed under CC BY 2.0.

to do her best and never gives up, even when things are hard. Things were difficult for her during the COVID-19 pandemic when she couldn't train at the gym. She had lists of exercises she did every day to train at home and weekly Zoom meetings with her coach. Friends of the family built some equipment including a space to hang a 10 foot rope and a floor bar. She had a growth spurt during that time and lost some of her skills, but she worked extra hard to get them back!

Arren's future goals are to go to the Olympics, be on the University of Cali-fornia gymnastics team and become a gym owner so she can coach other kids who love gymnastics as much as she does.

Do you have something you're passionate about? Arren wants you to know that through hard work and determination, you too can achieve your goals!

BECOME A

- **Follow your dreams.**
- **Encourage others to follow theirs too!**
- **You can follow Arren's journey on Instagram @tinygymnast_arren.**

ARREN'S ADVICE FOR YOU:

Stay true to yourself and follow through with the goals you want to accomplish. Success will come from putting in the work and believing in yourself.

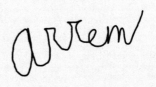

SHLOK

British Columbia, Canada

ANIMAL AMBASSADORS

"FIRST DONATE,
THEN INVEST,
AND THEN ENJOY."

Have you ever started or run your own business? When Shlok Chaitanya Parkhi was five years old, he wanted to start a business to make some money. His first idea was a lemonade stand, but his parents had another idea.

Because of his love for animals, his parents encouraged Shlok to use a Polaroid camera to take photos of people's pets. Since the pictures would come out of the camera instantly, Shlok could then charge people for the photos. He thought that was a great idea.

Shlok and his parents made a plan. His parents purchased the Polaroid camera and film. He and his mom made a poster that said "Pet Photos for $5.00". His mom started a page on Facebook to share his journey with others and help get the word out. Shlok's parents talked to him about spending his money wisely. They decided to split his **profits** three ways: he would **invest** some for his future, donate some to the local animal shelter, and spend some on something he wanted.

The next step was to get out and find pets to photograph. Shlok and his family started going for daily walks. They visited local dog parks and the beach. Shlok's confidence grew as he approached people asking if they would like a photograph of their pet. People were amazed at his courage and determination. Some wrote him thank you cards, some donated even more money, and many of them carried the pictures he took around with them all of the time.

This experience also taught Shlok how to handle rejection. Some people didn't want a photograph. That is life and Shlok learned that lesson and moved on gracefully. He met many new friends, both people and animals, and ended up taking 102 photographs in a month! He was able to donate more than $200 to the local animal shelter to help some kittens get their vaccinations.

Shlok plans on continuing his **entrepreneurial** efforts. In fact, he recently held a plant sale, sold over 100 plants, and donated money to the animal shelter again. Even though his plan was to make money for himself, he learned that giving back is important too. He used his passion to make a difference and you can too!

Your **PROFIT** is the money you make after you take out what you spent.

When you **INVEST**, you do something with your money to make it grow.

An **ENTREPRENEURIAL** effort organizes and operates a business.

SHLOK'S FUN FACTS:

- Shlok loves reading *Harry Potter* books.

- He can work on Lego sculptures tirelessly.

- Shlok loves golfing and riding horses.

- His favorite color is green because he loves nature.

BECOME A young CHANGEMAKERS™ ANIMAL AMBASSADOR!

SHLOK'S ADVICE FOR YOU:
Be consistent in your efforts!

- What do you like to do? Use your passions and talents to help others.

- Don't give up on your goals!

Shlok श्लोक

Shlok's signature written in Marathi, a language of the state of Maharashtra, India.

HAYLEY

Illinois, USA

HELPING HANDS

"STAY KIND!"

Most people think you need to be an adult in order to make a difference in the world and that you need to do something huge or spend a lot of money. People are wrong—there are young people who are taking small steps to solve problems every day! Hayley Orlinsky is one of them.

When Hayley was just seven years old and heard that hospitals were running out of masks and other **PPE** during the early stages of the **COVID-19 pandemic**, she was inspired to use her love of making friendship bracelets to help. Hayley decided to try to sell **Rainbow Loom** bracelets and donate the money to her local hospital.

The first thing she did was create a price list and samples of the bracelets. Hayley then created a video about her mission, showing the different samples and prices. Her mom posted it on social media. With friends, family and even strangers buying bracelets, it only took a few hours for her to fly past her original goal of $200! She set a new goal of $10,000. When she reached that, she pushed for another $10,000 and another. Her ultimate ending point was $50,000, which she never thought she'd meet. In her mind, she would be making a few hundred bracelets, but her mission grew so huge that it took over her entire house! Hayley's project went on for 14 months—that's when she reached her $50,000 goal.

Hayley could not have done this on her own. She taught friends and family how to make bracelets so they could help her fulfill orders. She created a video tutorial which they sent to people and even

Hayley's Fun Facts:

- Hayley has been dancing since she was 18 months old. She has done ballet, tap, hip hop, jazz funk, lyrical, contemporary and acro.

- Hayley wants to be a news anchor when she grows up so she can report on positive and uplifting stories.

- She is the oldest of three sisters.

PERSONAL PROTECTIVE EQUIPMENT (PPE) is specialized clothing or equipment worn to protect people against disease. It can include masks, gowns and gloves.

The **COVID-19 PANDEMIC** is a disease that was first seen at the end of 2019. It can cause mild to severe respiratory illness.

RAINBOW LOOM bracelets are made by weaving tiny elastic bands together.

taught people how to make the bracelets live over Zoom! She received gift cards from craft stores, such as Michael's and Joann Fabrics, to help pay for rubber bands. People donated funds and supplies. 400 kids and counselors at Hayley's summer camp also made bracelets. She came home with hundreds of bracelets every day! Hayley was inspired by everyone who stepped up to help her. Some celebrities even got involved in her cause! Drew Barrymore and Carrie Underwood each donated. After seeing Hayley on the television, her bracelets were featured in the official swag bags at the Grammy Awards!

The money Hayley's team raised for the hospital helped provide masks, and PPE to low-income families too! Even though it was hard work, Hayley never lost sight of why she was doing it. She made a difference and you can too!

BECOME A

young CHANGEMAKERS™ HELPING HAND!

- Do you enjoy making crafts or art? You could sell your art and donate the funds to a cause you care about.

- Buy crafts or art made by someone who is donating the money.

HAYLEY'S ADVICE FOR YOU:
Find something you love to do and see if there's a way to use it to help others. For example, if you like to paint or build with LEGO bricks, you can sell your creations to benefit a charity that's meaningful to you.

Hayley

LONDON
Maryland, USA

INSPIRATIONAL ICONS

"THE ONLY PERSON WHO CAN DEFEAT ME, IS ME. I AM THE ONLY PERSON WHO CAN STAND IN THE WAY OF WHAT I WANT. IT IS IMPORTANT TO BELIEVE THAT I CAN ACHIEVE ANYTHING MY HEART AND MIND WANT BECAUSE WHEN I BELIEVE AND SAY I CAN, THEN I WILL. WHEN I BELIEVE AND SAY I CAN'T, THEN I WON'T."

Have you ever heard of **Jiu-Jitsu**? It's a type of martial art based on ground fighting and holds. London Navarro learned all about it after she and her brother were being physically bullied at school.

When London was six and her brother was nine, people began to bully them. Her parents reported the bullying to the school several times, but unfortunately, the school did not believe them. London was then attacked by the boy who was bullying her brother and ended up in the hospital! That was when her parents started looking into enrolling London and her brother into martial arts and self-defense classes. They decided on Jiu-Jitsu. Little did they know what a huge impact this decision would have not only on London and her brother, but on many other children around the world too!

At first, London was nervous about taking the classes. She was going up against kids who were bigger, older and stronger than her, just like her bully. She was afraid she would be hurt. The other students and her instructor, however, made London feel comfortable

JIU-JITSU is perfect for self-defense and protection. It allows you to knock an opponent to the ground, which protects you and saves your opponent from harm. It was designed to help a smaller, weaker person defeat a larger, stronger opponent.

and were so supportive, that she thrived. She kept trying, she kept practicing and after a few months, London was beating kids who had been training longer than she had! After her first tournament she was hooked!

As London's journey into this new skill continued, her self-confidence grew. Her parents supported her every step of the way. They transferred London and her brother to a new school to give them a fresh start. Her dad eventually started taking Jiu-Jitsu classes too! Her parents, neighbors, classmates, instructors and other martial arts students helped London learn to believe in herself.

Jiu-Jitsu has changed London's life. She is now stronger, wiser, more confident, and more disciplined. She is proud of herself for turning a dark time in her life into something positive.

London's experience has also helped her community. People could see the change in her and signed their kids up for Jiu-Jitsu too! She and her brother demonstrated their skills at talent shows and London now helps teach Jiu-Jitsu at her current

Jiu-Jitsu academy. London has an Instagram account and has been on television. When other kids see London and her brother demonstrating their skills, they want to try this martial art too! She's heard from kids all over the world that they've joined Jiu-Jitsu because of her–this is the most rewarding part of the journey for London.

London's future plans include being a multi world black belt champion in Jiu-Jitsu. She would like to travel the world to learn from the best black belts, and bring self-defense classes into schools as an elective class. She would also like to open her own Jiu-Jitsu academy some day. London hopes her story will continue to inspire other kids out there who are going through a tough time. She wants them to know that if she can become a champion, they can too!

BECOME A young CHANGEMAKERS INSPIRATIONAL ICON!

- **Speak up for people being picked on.**

- **Be kind to others.**

- **Make a point to do something kind every day.**

ARREN'S ADVICE FOR YOU:
Being really smart is great but it's just as important to show compassion. If you see anyone being teased, name-called, or see something unfair and unjust, say something. Speak up, stand up for them or go to an adult in charge. A little gesture makes a big difference in someone's life.

London

LONDON'S FUN FACTS:

- **London loves sports. She plays basketball, wrestles, and wants to try lacrosse.**

- **Her favorite food is baked macaroni and cheese.**

- **Her favorite color is navy blue.**

- **London loves math and art.**

MELATI & ISABEL

Bali, Indonesia - - - - -

CONSERVATION CREW

"KIDS MIGHT BE ONLY 25% OF THE POPULATION, BUT THEY ARE 100% OF THE FUTURE."

Did you know that plastic NEVER goes away? Most people use plastic for about fifteen minutes and then the plastic sits on earth forever and often ends up in the ocean. When sisters Melati and Isabel Wijsen were 12 and 10 years old, they were inspired to do something about plastic pollution through a lesson they had at school about impactful world leaders such as Martin Luther King, Jr, and Nelson Mandela. That lesson left them wondering—what could they, as young people, do to make a difference?

An **NGO** (non-governmental organization) is a nonprofit organization that operates independently of any government, and usually tries to address a social or political issue.

A **PETITION** is a paper signed by many people to encourage the government to make a change.

LOBBYING is the act of trying to persuade governments to make decisions or support something.

The sisters began thinking about all of the issues their island of Bali in Indonesia was facing. One of the biggest problems was garbage. They noticed plastic washing in from the ocean and the rivers. It was clogging up the gutters and piling up in rivers, on the coast, and in fields. It was everywhere! In fact, the sisters found out that Indonesia is the world's second-largest source of marine plastic pollution, directly after China! The girls decided this was a problem they could do something about right now! They knew it was a huge challenge, so they had to think about a realistic goal that they, as kids, could meet.

After some research, they found out that dozens of countries around the world had already banned single-use plastic. If those countries could do it, they could do it too! They created their **NGO Bye Bye Plastic Bags (BBPB)** to raise awareness about plastic pollution, empower young people to take action and, ultimately, rid the world of plastic bags. They set up a Facebook page and asked their friends to help. Then they began spreading the word, which got more and more youth to help. They created **petitions**, led beach clean-ups, spoke at events and schools, provided cloth bags to shops, **lobbied** the government, and even at one point threatened a hunger strike to get the Bali governor's attention—all at the very young ages of 12 and 10 years old. They attended local markets, festivals and events, talking to others about the dangers of plastic, and handing out reusable bags.

On June 23, 2019, after six years of campaigning and meeting with lawmakers and other government officials, single-use plastic bags were banned in Bali—a huge victory for the country and for Melati and Isabel. Although it's against the law, many people are still using plastic bags, so BBPB continues to visit local shops to hand out cloth bags and to educate people about plastic pollution. Despite the girls' victory, Indonesia is still the second largest source of marine plastic pollution, so they are more determined than ever to keep campaigning.

Many young people around the world have asked the girls about their mission and how they've made a difference, so the sisters turned BBPB into a global movement. They now have close to 60 teams all over the world. They,

and other young people, have talked to over a million youth and created an educational booklet for elementary schools in Indonesia, which encourages young children to say "bye bye" to plastic bags.

Isabel and Melati are proof that age is just a number. If you see a problem in your community, take a step to make a difference. Stand up for what you believe in and use your voice!

ISABEL AND MELATI'S FUN FACTS:

- Isabel loves the color pink, tutus and Barbies. She enjoys dancing and being with friends.

- Melati loves to read, walk in nature and go to the beach.

- They both enjoy Asian food.

BECOME A young **CHANGEMAKERS** **CONSERVATION CREW MEMBER!**

- **Say no to plastic bags! Use cloth instead.**

- **Don't litter–pick up litter in your area.**

- **Recycle.**

- **Visit byebyeplasticbags. org to find out more!**

ISABEL AND MELATI'S ADVICE FOR YOU:

Never let anybody tell you that you are too young!

Isabel

STACY C. BAUER

A native of Minneapolis, MN, Stacy C. Bauer is a wife, teacher, mother of two and owner of Hop Off the Press—a publisher of quality children's books. Along with self publishing her own books, Stacy enjoys helping aspiring authors realize their dreams. She is hoping to inspire people around the world to make a difference with her newest endeavor, nonfiction book series *Young Change Makers*. For more information and to check out Stacy's other books, visit www.stacycbauer.com.

EMANUELA NTAMACK

Emanuela Ntamack is an artist and children's book illustrator, a beloved wife and mother. She is married to her Cameroonian husband Alix, and together they have two boys. She has been drawing continuously ever since she could hold a pencil. Growing up, she studied Art and Design in school and university. After she became a mother, she discovered her love for children's books illustrations. One of the biggest satisfactions of her work is when children—including her own—are inspired by the illustrations that she creates. She is thankful to God for the gift of art, and for the diversity and the beauty of Creation, which is a never-ending source of inspiration.

YOU CAN MAKE A DIFFERENCE!

We all have unique gifts and strengths. How can you use
your one-of-a-kind strengths to make a difference?

My unique gifts and strengths include: (These can include things such
as playing an instrument, cooking, painting, public speaking, being friendly...)

_____

_____

_____

_____

_____

I am passionate about: (a certain animal(s), helping small children or the
elderly, helping the environment in some way)

_____

_____

_____

_____

_____

MY IDEAS

Things I can do to use my strengths to make a difference in an area I am passionate about:

_____

_____

_____

_____

_____

_____

_____

You can use this space to draw your ideas!

MY ACTION PLAN

My idea/goal: _____

_____

_____

My first step: _____

_____

_____

Who I can ask for help if I need it: _____

_____

_____

What I need to get started: _____

_____

_____

My ultimate goal: _____

_____

_____

YOU _CAN_ DO THIS! YOU'RE NEVER TOO YOUNG TO MAKE A DIFFERENCE!

Made in United States
North Haven, CT
07 February 2024

48144474R00024

KIDS AROUND THE WORLD
ARE DOING EXTRAORDINARY THINGS!

Chasing your dreams takes courage and passion, determination and a belief in yourself. In this book you'll meet 12 inspiring young people who set out to follow their dreams. They faced obstacles along the way but never gave up. By asking questions, making plans and following through, these young people made their big dreams come true, and their stories just might encourage you to follow your dreams too!

"I found myself getting teary eyed reading this book because of the amazing things these kids do for others. It's incredibly inspirational AND the educational bits for each child's cause are so informative! Well done!"

HEATHER E. ROBYN, ED.D.

"Well written, engaging and inspiring book which the students in my school will love. The way Stacy writes is engaging and accessible to all. The diversity of the ideas and youngsters as well as the inclusive nature of the book means it will appeal to everyone."

MS. FIONA M COLLINS
TEACHER LIBRARIAN

"The *Young Change Makers* series is brilliant! Seeing how the children featured in the series are changing the world (in big and small ways) inspires other children, and even adults, to reach out and be a force for good around them! I love recommending them to other parents and teachers!"

CARLA JANSEN
BEST-SELLING AUTHOR, HOMESCHOOLING MOM, AND TEACHER

Be sure to check out these books
in the *Young Change Makers* series!

WWW.STACYCBAUER.COM